STOP GROWING OLD IN LIFE

The 8 Habits to Grow Life

Brian Jones

CONTENTS

GROWTH
Starts Here

The **8 Habits to Grow Life** are the starting points to a grander vision for life. There has never been a greater time in history than now to take advantage of the knowledge at our fingertips to grow life.

Growth is built into our DNA as human beings, and we can grow and evolve throughout our lives until our last breathe on earth if we chose.

We all possess extraordinary powers, yet we fall short in many instances, never growing into who we were meant to be. Why is this? Is there ever a ceiling to growth, or do we stop short without pushing ourselves further?

William James, the great American Philosopher in the mid-1800's writes

"The human individual thus lives usually within his limits. He possess powers of various sorts, which he habitually fails to use. He energizes below his maximum, and he behaves below his optimum."

James observation in the mid-1800s compared to today, has much changed?

If you want a great life, you grow a great life. If you want a mediocre life, then you grow a mediocre life. If you want a safe life, you live within the walls of your safe life that is the life you live. This is cause and effect and what you put in is what you get out.

Growth of any life takes work. It can't be handed to you on a silver platter. You need a road map and a compass to know where you are going, grit and determination to get you through the challenges, and then continue in life to ask the right questions.

**Growth is a muscle
you need to exercise it all the time.**

Growth encompasses such a vast spectrum of life, yet when we break it down into sizeable chunks, we begin to identify that not all growth parts are the same. Not all aspects of growth will grow at the same speed.

You could grow your mind intellectually yet not grow your body. A doctor is growing his medical practice and not growing his health, eventually becomes a patient for the future. You could grow to have a six-pack and ignore the growth of the environment you continually put yourself in. Growth is everywhere when we train ourselves where to look.

**As the owners of life, it becomes our job
to steer our growth in the direction we desire.**

A few years ago, I was introduced to a three-word phrase by my nephew, which completely changed how I assess life. He blurted out **Grow or Die,** and I have latched on to that phrase ever since. I have added two more references that help guide me for quick answers. These are the questions I use to determine growth in my life.

**Grow or Die
Forward or Backward
Life can only travel in one direction at a time**

The first two phrases **grow or die** and **forward or backward**, I rely on for a quick YES or NO answer. Is my life growing in this area, or am I maintaining and slowly dying? YES or NO! Is my life moving forward in my actions, or am I going backward? YES or NO.

I don't want to get mired down in details at first I'm looking for quick answers. It will become evident in the future, where I put my efforts to grow in the areas I need to grow.

Life can only travel in one direction at a time. This is a quick reminder of which way I am heading in this area of life because you cannot be heading in two directions simultaneously. **SIMPLE AND DIRECT**

Stop Growing Old in Life becomes the starting point to a grander vision for life. You have an opportunity to get better at life little by little as you grow life. Every day you are not getting older you are growing. When we look at life through these eyes, we see a completely different picture.

No one wants to get old, yet we can all grow if we chose to. Take out the word age and replace it with grow. We are now giving a different set of instructions for the mind to follow!

If we never grow past our limiting beliefs, we will never see the other side where the juice of life exists. When you become your age as society has determined, we become a victim of our future capabilities.

Sometimes we have to **STOP,** put the brakes on step back from our minds, thoughts and actions, and assess, are we living the best possible life we can?

When you read over **The 8 Habits to Grow Life**, each habit represents a particular area of life. It is best to digest the information first, then question everything. Questions are what open the curiosity of life and point you in the direction of growth.

The word habit gets mixed up with a redundant set of routines that habitually run people's lives. They become automatic programs run in the subconscious mind. If they are good habits, that is good, and if they are bad habits, that is bad.

When I refer to a habit, my definition is an action you take in a specific direction that is always growing. I want to grow my habits, not get trapped inside them. Growing habits become addictive because you begin to notice the doors in life opening for you.

Knowing where you are today is just as important as where you are going tomorrow and where you have been.

The 8 Habits to Grow Life are the tools I use to grow my life. I ask the right questions for direction. I monitor my growth through constant feedback, and then I take the necessary actions to keep my life growing forward.

Once you understand that life is a process of many moving parts, there are so many ways you can grow in life. Limits will never hold you back. We have one shot here on earth, so why not make it our best life possible.

We can grow into who we were meant to be!

HABITS
of
Growth

**What are The 8 Habits to Grow Life, and
why do we need them in our life?**

L et's be honest we live in a world of abundance, and it is everywhere we choose to look. We don't lack for anything we have enough air to breathe, Energy from the sun, water to drink, clothes on our back, shelter, and food to eat. We get to live on this beautiful jewel of a planet we call earth. Once we realize how fortunate we are, we can get on with growing our lives!

Growing our lives is built into our DNA as human beings, yet the strength of that growth and that growth vary significantly between each individual.

What is Growth?

Growth is what you are doing and where you are going with your life. It is an ongoing process of developing one's self into something greater. Every life has a direction, and no two lives could ever be the same. You are growing forward inside your life as you go through life, or you end up maintaining life with not much growth for life. Without growth, you slowly start dying inside.

**When you focus on growing life
you are not focused on growing older**

that is what people who are growing older do!

When you have a direction and are growing, your age does not matter, you are building a better version of you. Who you were last week, last month, last year is not the same person you are today. Of course, everyone is getting older, yet some people grow throughout their lives and become ageless. Then some people grow older in life and become their age.

The words you use to describe life have a significant impact on the interpretation you give your life.

I am growing my life!
I am growing older!

They are words, yet the mind hears everything. If you tell yourself you are growing life, you are growing. If you tell yourself you are getting older, you become older. Your mind has to be clear on what you want!

Both lives are moving forward, yet the experiences and the outcomes of each life will be drastically different.

A life that is continuously moving forward in growth and actions is associated with change. You become a river of change. You are working with the natural flow of the river and not against it. Change is where you experience life. You live in the unknowns of life.

A Life that has stopped growing is now at its peak with little change for the future. Life directly converts to maintaining life, and you become a caretaker for life. Every day is exactly like the previous day, and if you are not changing, you are not growing, and if you are not growing, you will never experience the life you could have lived. You live in the knowns of life where it is safe.

"Don't go through life, grow through life"
Eric Butterworth

Grow or Die

To better understand our existence in life, sometimes we have to look outside ourselves to discover the clues to what the rest of the universe is doing.

Step outside your front door and just observe what is transforming before your eyes. Look around your backyard or up in the sky, everything is growing, creating, and evolving, or it is slowly dying. If it can't recreate itself into a better version of itself, then it will become extinct. That is the fundamentals of life, and it is being played out in every corner of the universe.

Nature and all its entities are well organized and have a definite purpose for their existence. They know where they stand in the hierarchy of life, so they are left to evolve over millions and millions of years. The evolutionary process stops when they can't adapt to the ever-changing environment.

If we look at human life, why would we think we would be any different?

If we don't evolve as a species, what are the chances we will be around for the next ten thousand years? If we can't grow as human beings, what are the chances we live a long life?

In the grand scheme of time on this planet, we are only taking our baby steps compared to cosmological time. Time on this planet as a human being is limited to what you put into life.

When everything else in the universe is in creation growth, I think it would be a good idea to follow the universe as it has been at this game a little longer than we have.

Think of a rocket ship as it takes off from earth into outer space it has unlimited possibilities where it can go. The scenery is forever changing as it hurdles its way through space.

Your life as a rocket ship is heading in a definite direction as it is always moving forward into the unknown. You have unlimited time unlimited space until one day it finally runs out of Energy.

7

You are growing strong until the end.

An airplane takes off, growing in altitude with a definite direction and destination in place. Once the level of height is reached, it is now at its highest peak.

As an airplane, your life starts strong with lots of gas in the tank yet reaches a point where it maintains an altitude and speed and coasts on autopilot until it has to descend to its final destination. You have lots of gas left in the tank for another flight to another destination, but life has other plans, and you can't go any further. Your life and an airplane are held back by the rules and limitations. Suitable for the plane yet not too good for you to experience life.

**You can be a rocket ship or an airplane
There is no right or wrong answer, just two ways to live life.**

The 8 Habits of Growth are designed to take a section of life and quickly determine whether you are growing life or not. These habits are based on the observations of life and how we can learn from everything around us.

- **Grow or die** – which way is your life heading?
- **Choice** – your life is made up of thousands and thousands of choices
- **Creation** – you are the creation of your life?
- **Environment** – You decide on the environment for your life
- **Feedback loop** – noticing what is working and what is not
- **Mindset** - do you have a growth mindset or a fixed mindset
- **Evolution** - Is your life evolving or revolving?
- **Health** – Health care is growing health into a better version of yourself.

To grow or die is a choice.

The **creation** of a **mindset** is in an **environment** you chose.
The **evolution** is in the **feedback loop**
which grows your **health**.

Three types of people in this world

Some people can grow throughout their entire lives. They give all they can into their life and try to leave no stone unturned. They can take their final breath with no regrets. These are the people who keep reinventing themselves, living in a constant state of change, growing into a better version of themselves all the time.

Others will grow until their basic needs have been met. They maintain and put their life on an automatic program, never pushing themselves past their limiting beliefs. They fear change far greater than to grow life. They focus on stability, where there is no growth and no change.

Finally, some people grow their lives up until a specific point and then stop their growth with a premature stop date. Society is telling them to go off and reward themself for a life well-lived. When you stop your growth, you begin to lose the purpose of life. Whatever your purpose was up until that point stops, and if you don't reinvent yourself, you become a caretaker for life.

Life is Energy and growth is Energy, and when it stops, it stops.

Do you think Oprah Winfrey is thinking about stopping the growth of her life? Bill Gates keeps reinventing himself repeatedly. Do you think he is counting the days when he can stop his Philanthropy endeavors?

Warren Buffet, 90, and **Charlie Munger,** 96, of Berkshire Hathaway, are not counting the days when they can finally sit on a beach and count their successes. Their entire life is how they judge success. To stop what they have been doing and growing would go against what has kept them alive.

These are choices in life, and each one will lead you on a different trajectory of life.

The 8 Habits to Grow Life are guideposts to give you a path to choose an opening of ideas of how you can grow life. Not everyone is designed to grow life because of limiting beliefs and routines we get stuck inside. A habit of growth is a habit you can develop throughout your life.

After reading many books on the growth of life, it becomes evident that you grow an extraordinary life if you want to have an extraordinary life.

After each chapter, have a reflection on what it means to you. Simply ask is my life growing in this area or not—no need to over-analyze.

I like to incorporate growing habits where they are always evolving throughout my life. I'm am pushing myself a little farther each time to get the most out of life. When you are growing, you are getting better at life a little bit at a time. You end up at the end of your life and say, holy crap look what I've accomplished.

If you are to follow anything in life, the universe, which is continuously expanding, is a great role model. Cheers, enjoy the book, Brian

GROW OR DIE

Life!

Is your life growing, or is it dying?

W hat does a growing life look like? What does a dying life look like? Do you believe you have a choice in which direction your life will travel?

These are huge questions in a world filled with answers, opinions, behaviors, actions, ultimately deciding which side of life we would like to participate in. This never-ending wheel of information is found everywhere, but the truth is always best when it comes from within you and from your actions.

Do you believe the outside world will determine your destiny?
OR
Do you believe that you determine your destiny?

Questions that challenge our thinking, alter our thoughts, and open our minds can uncover layers of past beliefs layered over time to protect us from ourselves. When taken off, the rose-colored glasses can reveal a new world and path for your future.

Having ahhha moments is what we need from time to time to spark the curiosity of what a life can become. The growth of your future is now dependent on the path you choose. Not all paths are equal, as is each life lived.

I like to think that each life has a direction, and ultimately, we **choose** that direction. We have two paths to take, we can grow life, or we can die inside life. We can live with possibilities or limitations. We can turn left or right, go up or down or in and out, yet we can only choose one direction at a time.

You have been driving your car for miles down this road we call life, and it finally comes to a stop. You have a decision to make, do I turn left or do I turn right because each direction changes your life's dynamics forever.

Your road of life has been a growing and discovering adventure so far. Living and opening the doors, challenging yourself, and moving forward at every level of life. Each step forward has been rewarded with a small shot of dopamine (Life's Reward Chemical) into your system as a reminder for all your hard work. Your life has been growing and traveling in one definite direction.

Turn left, and you continue down this road of never-ending growth and potentials. You continue living in the unknowns uncovering possibilities that are everywhere. You widen your comfort zone where you feel alive and grow into who you were meant to be.

Turn right you are now at the top of your growth cycle of life. You put your life on autopilot and will never realize your true potential. In essence, you resort to maintaining life as a caretaker for your life. You are growing older in life.

Grow or Die

So let's define what a growing life means vs a dying life and see how we can further differentiate between the two.

Growing Life
- You have a **vision** for your **future** and are not focused on your past
- You have a **growth mindset**
- You **think, act** and **become** your **future**
- Your **commitment** to **growth** is until your **last breath** on **earth**
- **Each day** becomes a **new adventure**
- you want to become **greater than yesterday**

- You refer as **I am growing** in life
- You realize what makes you **uncomfortable** makes you **grow**

Dying Life

- You are the **story** of your **past** and where you have come from
- You have a **fixed mindset**
- Your **thoughts actions** are **representative** of your past
- You **maintain life** as you move forward in life
- **Each day** is the **same** as the day before
- Your **best days** are **behind you**
- You refer as **I am aging** in life
- You realize that you prefer to be **comfortable** and **maintain** life

We get to choose everything in our lives, and that also includes the direction of our life. Step back for a minute and think about this fact. We can decide how we interpret every single event and make all the decisions about those events. We decide if we let words hurt us or become bulletproof to others opinions. Use success and failure as a chance to learn or a chance to be judged.

These events can spin our world out of control or challenge us in our beliefs and grow past the possibilities in life. One life, you become the victim of life, and the other, you become the victor of life. Each one has an eventual direction attached, and you get to decide which train you would like to hop on.

When we are growing, we are growing there is nothing too complicated in this realization. When we are dying, we are dying again there is nothing complicated in this fact. They are merely directions of life, yet they hold the keys to your future and have dramatic effects on the way we experience life.

Picture someone who is growing life and discovering themselves and the world around them. Expanding their footprint and putting their stamp on the world. Their life would consist of opening doors, reaching for opportunities, living in potentials and possibilities, and making all their wishes and desires come true. Their future is bright and is heading in a particular direction.

Picture someone who is dying they have resolved to the fact that their better years are behind them. They no longer have that drive and ambition to grow life; instead, they maintain and become a caretaker for life. Their past now becomes their most significant achievement.

In one instant, we are picturing someone who has their life in front of them to grow and the other who has stopped the growth of their life. So tell me, who is who? What age would each life represent?

What is so interesting with these questions is we would automatically assume that the younger person is growing life and the older person is the aging life. What if the older person is the growing life and the younger person is the aging life?

If you are ten, twenty, forty, sixty eighty or one hundred and still growing, you are becoming greater in life. Why would you stop growing? You have established growth as a positive habit for life. What is age at this point, or is it a number to judge ourselves against other people? If you are growing life, do you think age is that important or is your life's growth more critical?

You could be thirty and stop growing and just maintain life for the next fifty years. Are you growing life, or are dying inside life. Which life sounds like the kind of life you want to live? Do you think ten years of growth would far outweigh fifty years of no growth?

Age is age, and growth is growth
when you stop growing, you become your age
you slowly start to die.

What if we never stopped growing life?

Who says we have to stop?

Who are the people who have taught us this way of thinking?

These are all societal dogmas that get brainwashed inside our heads and start to limit our potential in life. Where is that transformational point when life shifts from a Growing life to a Dying life?

**A growing life keeps you young at heart and gets you out of bed every morning.
A dying life is the snooze button on the alarm clock.**

If a growing life is established when we are growing moving forward with our actions, then a dying life would be cemented when we stop growing, and our efforts are now of maintaining life. When we stop growing, we start dying there is no other alternative.

Nature and all its entities have lived and breathed their existence for millions and millions of years. They grow, they die if that they can't evolve into something greater at that time, they become extinct there is nothing complicated in that sentence. The evidence is everywhere we chose to look. If we fail to realize this fact, then we become poor observers of life.

When do the wheels stop turning on your life?

In my last working adventure, I was a salesman, traveled to thousands of companies, and met many friendly people. Some of them loved their job, and others hated their job, and others were just on autopilot somewhere in the middle. Every so often, someone would come up to me and announce, hey Brian, I'm retiring. My response was always the same. So what are you going to do with your life now?

My observations over the years have never changed. The people who loved their job also had plans for the next stage of life and would elaborate quite extensively. They had an energy about growing their life and their future, and I could see it.

The people who were just there in the middle had some idea where they were going, yet most were happy to retire. The people who hated their jobs response was usually the same, getting the hell away from this place.

Merely an observation from many years of observations. Yet I think a good indication of where each life was going.

I have always worked for myself, so I have decided what I do for a living. I've had some great years in business and life and some bad ones. The great times were when I was growing my life, my business, and the money flowed. The bad times were also when I stopped growing my life became comfortable, business became difficult, and the money dried up.

I always enjoyed what I did, yet I never loved what I was doing. There is a vast difference.

I made a huge decision ten years ago that completely changed the trajectory of my life forever. I met my wife, and my daughter got married and built a house in Thailand. I went from maintaining my life at that time to growing life in an instant, and that hasn't stopped because I haven't allowed it to stop.

When you decide to live in a new country, adopt a new culture, and view the world through a new set of eyes, you begin to grow your life in so many ways. I did not want to take my ideas of Canada's life, which was fabulous, and transplant them into Thailand. I am committed to growing my life, and when you commit to growing, you grow in all areas of life to best experience life.

Today from my house in Thailand, I am a writer of books, music, podcaster, running a publishing company rice farmer, meditating daily, spending two hours reading and studying new ways to grow mentally and physically. I am also on a quest to live to 120 years of age naturally, so Longevity in life is vital. I wrote a book about it called **Longevity Starts Now!**

I am busier than ever, yet I feel I'm doing what I was meant to do with my life. This is not work I'm living my passion with a purpose, and I awake motivated to the moon to keep growing my life forward every day.

One of my friends messaged me the other day and asked about my retirement plans, concerned I was working so much that I didn't have time to enjoy my life in Thailand.

My answer was
"I'm doing what I love, why would I stop?"
"I have a plan and a purpose for my life why would I stop?"
"It gives me a reason to get out of bed, why would I stop?"

He didn't have a reply and wished me luck.

That doesn't mean I become a work acholic sleep fours a night, ignore my family, no holidays. It means when I work; I work when it is family time its family time. When it's time for sleep, I sleep. When it's time for a holiday, I am entirely on holiday. When I talk with my daughter, I am 100% focused with attention on my daughter. Why would I stop the very thing that's keeping me alive?

When you have a passion in life and get to live it, and then you turn that passion into a purpose, you have just been given the keys to your life. A passion is what you are doing in life, and a purpose is the reason you are doing what you are doing. These two together intrinsically aligned transforms any life into a growing life. **Direction!**

Your whole life becomes the journey. If there are stoppages, they just become speedbumps along the way. Why would you stop? **Direction!**

When you have a growing life, it doesn't have a temporary stop date in the future. You see where you are going, not where you've been. You are focused on the creations in life and how to grow them. **Direction!**

The doors of life are open, not closed. You are not afraid to make choices that can alter your path growing forward. You live in the unknowns and take on life challenges continuously. You are becoming more comfortable about being uncomfortable in life. **Direction!**

The idea is to continue on the growth curve as a lifetime commitment. **Direction!**

So when is that moment that your life stops growing?

Think of life as a giant clock, and twelve o'clock represents the start and finishing time of life. Where on this clock are the hands of your life if the average lifespan is eighty. Every three hours represents twenty years. Is your life growing right now or not. Does time fly by, or is it standing still? Every minute is a new adventure, or does each minute look the same. When one hour goes by, are you saying, ohh my goodness, look what I have accomplished, or are you saying, where did the time go?

Some people can grow their life until the last breath at 11:59, then close their eyes and say goodbye. Other people stop their growth around three o'clock and now maintain a life for the next sixty years. The next group grows until their necessities are met in life and become protectors of their possessions, not pushing themselves any farther. Life goes on autopilot

The timeframe and growth become different for everyone, yet the results can have huge implications on how we live our lives.

My studies on Longevity have brought me around to discover

many trends in life.

When I observe people from all walks of life, you see the same pattern in varying degrees. People who have a passion and a purpose and grow their lives tend to live longer lives.

The people from **Okinawa, Japan,** have more centurions than other places on earth. They continuously live longer lives, free from most illnesses and diseases. They live a clean and healthy lifestyle and usually work right up until they die. In their vocabulary, they don't have a word for retirement. They **grow** their lives throughout their life.

Bill Gates, in his second life after Microsoft, is transforming the world of philanthropy. Along with his wife Melinda, they tackle some of the world's most pressing issues like poverty, vaccines, water, third world problems, and now the coronavirus. Their lives are about **growing**, learning, and giving back through The Giving Pledge.

Warren Buffet and **Charlie Munger** run one of the most successful companies in the world Berkshire Hathaway. Warren is Ninety, and Charlie is Ninety Six. As the company **grows**, they **grow**. Ask them about retirement they'll they'd probably insult you for asking such a stupid question. They are still **growing** their lives they haven't got time to get old in their lives.

A ninety-year-old man with his six buffalo walks by my house every day on his way to the rice fields. A rice field becomes a great place to feed the buffalo when the rice is not in season. One day I asked the man through my wife translating, **"why doesn't he get his son to help him with his buffalo"** his response, **"The buffalo need to be fed,"** and off he went down the path.

His response was not what I was expecting, yet if I had been a better observer of life, I would have realized the answer before I even asked the question. Feeding the buffalo doesn't transform the world, yet it changes his world. He is still **growing** in his life with a reason to get out of bed. I still have so much more to learn about life.

Examples of life

- To live an **extraordinary life**, it takes **extraordinary measures** inside your life
- To live a **great life**, it takes **great actions** inside your life
- To live a **growing life**, it takes **growing your creations** inside your life
- To live an **ordinary life**, it takes **ordinary actions** inside your everyday life
- To **maintain life** is to **maintain the same life** day after day
- To live a **dying life** is to **grow older** in life

A Growing Habit

Life can develop into growing habits where everything becomes about growth. Your creations, mind, health, and finally, your freedom are all tied into growth. You have developed systems over time designed to always point you in the direction you are heading.

A habit is just a redundant set of patterns you do over and over where the body knows it as well as your mind. In growth, you are always slipping into the habit of growth in your actions, moving you forward in your thoughts, behaviors, and emotions.

- Your creations never stop growing they become the process of your life. The more you grow your creations, the more your life grows.
- Your mind is in a constant state of growing knowledge and learning—you challenging yourself more and more, building your belief into what is possible inside a life. The only person that can stop you is you.
- Health is taking full responsibility for your health and

growing it. You believe in health care vs sick care. A day doesn't go by where you are not aware of how you feel and react to life elements. You become an active participant in your health.

- Freedom becomes the frequency of your life, a rhythm where there are no boundaries, only possibilities. What you grow, you become, they are aligned.

If we go back to the beginning of this chapter and ask the question, is your life growing, or is it dying, what would your answer be?

There is no right or wrong, only different levels of life where anyone can participate. We can change the direction of any life from a growing life to a dying life instantly. We can also change a dying life into growing life just as fast.

Your mindset becomes the key to this transformation because the mind that created the direction in the first place will also be the mind that changes the direction.

Be very clear on what you want for your life, and take the necessary steps to change. Follow some of the outlines I have expressed here and grow.

You eventually will become the direction of your life!

When you apply **The 8 Habits to Grow Life**, it is like a compass to determine which direction you are heading quickly. These three words can apply to so many of life's situations because, in a few seconds, you can get a quick and accurate indication about your life minus all the baggage.

Is my life growing?
Or
Is my life dying

Choose wisely your life could depend on it!

CREATION

We can live in Creation our entire lives!

W e can create as we move through life, or we can exist inside the creation. Yes, we are the creation. Our lives are the creation, and we get to grow this creation into whatever we want, desire, or wish. There are no limits to create, only the limits we put on to ourselves.

We can spend ten years, half our life, or our entire life, building this creation if we choose to. We can also decide not to create and accept what life has to offer.

There is no right or wrong in either decision because this becomes a choice as to which path we choose, yet when we are creators, we are working with the universe's natural laws, which is the real creation.

So what is a creation at the fundamental core?

It is the act or process of bringing something into existence. When we think of creation, is your mind leaning towards a vision, passion, job career relationship business, or anything representing a creation? These are all creations, yet to understand creation properly, we need to take a step back and view it with a different set of eyes.

These are good starting points, but only the branches of a tree, not where we begin. The very core where an actual creation starts is not found outside you it starts within you first. You are your creation. Your creation has to start with you first.

When you realize where the starting gate is, as I like to call it, the launching pad, you have the opportunity to grow this creation into whatever you want for as long as you would like. Until the end of your life would be a goal, add one more day to give it some real zest for life.

Building anything that lasts a lifetime must be rooted deep into the ground like a tree. A tree is only as healthy as the root system that anchors it to the ground.

When the wind blows, it only blows and doesn't topple over the tree of creation. When it rains, it rains and feeds the tree with nutrients to help it grow. When the sun shines, it gives the tree energy to flourish in this world. There is nothing too complicated here. Life and creation is what it is.

Nature and all the entities that call earth home understand their existence, and they all work in cooperation. When we realize they have been in creation for millions and billions of years, we should be paying close attention to their existence to learn more about our existence on this planet we call earth.

When they stop creating, they become extinct. If they can't recreate themselves into a better version of themselves that is adapting to a new environment, they become extinct.

Creation can be as simple as if you are not in creation, you are dying.

Life can only travel in one direction at a time. Creation becomes the direction for your life!

Creation is what you do with your life. Your life's creation starts with you, then I can create with the skills I have been given. For everyone on this planet, it is different.

You could start in your working life as a Fireman, thinking that this is your true calling. Every day you love to go to work because of the challenges and rewards the job provides you. In your mind, you are doing what you were meant to do in life.

In your spare time, you also love to do projects around your home. You love it and are good at it. Your family and friends are so impressed they want you to post videos of the process on Youtube so they can learn the skills as well. It also gives you a chance to connect with them all.

Wouldn't you know, in three months, you have 1000 subscribers following you on Youtube because they find you and your projects interesting. You create a new video every few weeks for your family and friends, not realizing other people find this interesting as well.

Over the year, you have subscribers worldwide tuning in to your channel waiting for your next project. Your subscription base has grown exponentially, and now this hobby you loved so much has turned into a new creation of yourself all because you allowed the creative process to evolve.

Justin Beiber, the international Pop superstar, started out singing in front of the Avon Theatre in downtown Stratford Ontario Canada. His family in other parts of the country wanted to hear him sing as well. So he decided to shoot some videos of him singing and playing guitar and put them on YouTube.

Scooter Braun, a talent scout, found one of his videos and signed him to a contract, and the rest is history. This all happened because he was just following the creative process at the time.

The creation process can simply start as a simple yes to something, and off it goes into directions you would never have imagined. Yes, to life yes to a new creation, yes, a new avenue of life.

The creation of life has no limits, only the limits we put onto ourselves. When you are in the creative process, it sends signals to your body that says my life is open to what the universe has in store. What a beautiful way to go through life!

What sets us apart from anything else on the planet is our brain. Not just any brain, thinking, doing, being, brain. It can create invent, it has intention, can process vast amounts of data, reason freewill, learn advanced skills, and so much more. We can create our life. This is far different than anything else on the planet.

We have been on earth for a mere two hundred thousand years. In the cosmic timetable, we are just taking our first breaths and baby steps on our journey.

Our ultimate game of life will be to see if we can evolve as a species for the next million years. With a brain advanced as we have, will we create ourselves right off the planet into extinction?

Creation is a double-edged sword when you have a brain like we do and time to kill.

I believe we were born into this world as creators of our life and not caretakers for life. Why else are we here? We can over-analyze everything and try to think of our importance to the grandness of the universe, yet we are truly a dust particle on top of a dust particle in the universe's grand scope.

We got to this point as human beings as a creation of something. If everything else around us is creating for their survival, existence, or extinction, it should make sense we follow the path of least resistance and follow the universe—move-in the direction you want for your life.

When we can view our existence at the quantum level, everything in the universe is made of all the same stuff to varying degrees. When we realize this fact and see it for what it is, we can concentrate our energy on creating our life.

We are creators, not caretakers for life.

We were put on this earth **not** to occupy space but to **create** and **evolve** as a species.

Grow your Creation

You become your creation!

Growing your creation is as fundamental as the creation itself. A bicycle has wheels, a creation has growth. Ice cream tastes great, and creation has growth. Kim Kardashian has......... I will have to work on this one, and creation has growth. When you create, you grow, and when you grow, you create.

Once the wheels of life start moving, it is hard to stop the forward motion; they are intrinsically aligned. We can begin with an intention for this creation, giving it a reason for its existence: the fuel it needs through motivation to accelerate the train of life as it leaves the station.

Life should be a journey of creations growing at every level and not bound by limitations that hold us back from our potential. We have an opportunity to grow relentlessly through the good, bad, and the ugly that life can throw at us.

A deeply rooted creation will not be sidetracked by life events or happens; they will just be adjustments along the road of life. If your creation is for a lifetime, all these separate events only become events. Your creation and growth are what you do, and your actions are what you control as you move forward in life.

When we see our life as a creation, we can begin to understand the early signs of mastering the game of life. When we master ourselves, we hold all the power. When we have all the power, we will never become a prisoner inside life. This is real power, which is not designed around power over others, only power over yourself. You are your creation!

I had a conversation with a friend of mine the other day about growing life as a creation of yourself. Why? To me, it is a fascinating concept to think about. Let me repeat that TO ME.......

It was kind of a one-way conversation as I was talking, he was listening. He seemed kind of interested, yet not many words had escaped from his mouth. REALLY NICE WOW HMMM Then finally came the six words as a response "sounds like a lot of work."

At the time, I was dumbfounded by the reaction, yet I soon discovered that I was in the minority about my importance for growing life to create yourself.

First, you have to wrap your head around the concept, and that takes time. **Second,** it does sound like you are adding a new layer of life onto a life that is already busy with life. **Third,** go back to the first one.

Growing your creation is pointing your life in the direction you want to head and making the proper choices that reinforce your life direction and saying yes to life!

To be a caretaker for life, you are shutting the door on your life's creative process. You are telling the universe that life at this present moment is not about growing or experiencing new possibilities it is about maintaining an existence.

If you are not growing life, then you are dying inside life. Life only travels in one direction at a time! When we observe the universe and nature, they are the guideposts along the way of life. To ignore their presence and be blind to their purpose is to go against the natural laws of life that govern everything in the universe.

Stagnation

What is stagnation?

Stagnation at every level is anti-life, it holds you back from your true potential and life possibilities. The root of stagnation is the Latin word for "standing water." A flowing river is alive and ever-changing, and stagnation is a pond with standing water where a mosquito hangs out, ready to take a bite out of life.

When you grow your creation, you are evolving, life is happening you are in the flow, yet when you start to slow down life and drift into the maintenance of a life, you are now entering stagnation.

> **"Stagnation is death**
> **If you don't change you die**
> **It's that simple it's that scary"**
> Leonard Sweet

Let's break down these three lines in this Leonard Sweet quote because they are such powerful reminders about life. When you analyze each line and their meanings, we begin to understand the devastating effects of stagnation on a life.

"Stagnation is death" are harsh words to hear, yet when you start to think about the magnitude of these three words and how they apply to life, we can better understand where we stand on our journey.

Nature is our real teacher in life and a guide for us to follow. What happens to a flower when it stops growing? It dies, it is that simple. When it is growing, it is supple, moist, alive it is in creation using the sun's energy, soil, and water.

When a flower stops its creation and growth cycle, it starts the process of slowly dying. The energy is now depleting, it's lifeless as it whittles, becomes brittle, and begins to die.

When we look at nature and all her creations, they are all governed by the same rules. When we analyze the Universe and its inhabitants, they all follow the same patterns.

When they are not growing and creating for their existence in life, they die and become extinct. No creation just exists to exist; they are constantly traveling in one direction.

So when we apply the word stagnation to a human life, we soon realize maintaining a life is stagnation. If you are not creating or growing your life, you are dying inside life, as brutal as that might sound. Yet this is how the universe and nature have operated for billions of years.

How many people do you know just live their lives without any thought of growing and creating their lives?

We have never been taught this way of thinking in our society. Most ideologies are rooted in the maintenance of a life vs the creation and growth of life.

"To be the true creator of life, this requires a lifetime commitment."

"If you don't change, you die" This second line is a reminder of how important it is always to have a pulse on your life. You have to become aware of where you are on your journey in life. When you are stuck in stagnation, you might not realize, because it comes in the form of maintaining your existence in life.

When you look around your neighborhood, everyone is living and doing the same thing, so it must be the way forward for life.

If you get up every morning and do the same thing for the next five ten-twenty years without any change, you are in stagnation.

We think 60 to 70 thousand thoughts every day, yet the problem arises when we realize 90% of those thoughts are the same as the day before. Has your life changed at all that day, week, month, or year?

When we reach 30-35 years of age, most of our habits and routines have been established for our lives. We enter the next stage of life. This is where the stagnation of life can take hold of you and never let you go. If you are not growing and creating life after this point, you are now entering stagnation.

When the past is now your future, and you have stopped having a future brighter than your past and stop the natural flow of life, you are now in stagnation.

When you stop the cycle of creation and growth, you are now waiting for life to dictate to you. Standing still means it becomes easy to get run over by life and its happenings. When we stop reaching for the next rung on the ladder of life, we are saying to the Universe......

Hey Universe .... I have gone as far as this life is going to take me.
Or
We can recognize the signs, learn to adapt,
and move forward with our life.

"It's that simple, it's that scary." Society teaches us many things, some good and some bad, yet when we lose our free will to think for ourselves, we haven't learned anything about our existence here on earth.

Example
We teach systems in society designed around maintaining life, not around the creation and growth of life. From grade one on to College and University, most of society is taught from a system designed in the 1800s.

We are worried about the grades people get, diplomas they have, resumes they present, and their job interview skills. We have been programmed to believe that this is the measuring stick we have for success in life. That is short term thinking and only grades for rewards and achievements.

Today most people still go to school to get a job to do that job for the next 30-40 years until it is time to retire. The only problem is the job you're at right now might not be around in the future.

Technology has changed the landscape of our future forever. We have to change and adapt to the new realities that we face as technology changes, so do we or we get left behind; this is the new paradigm we face today.

If we can teach at an early age that creating your life and learning is the path forward, we take responsibility for our lives. Grades are ok, yet the process of creation, growth, and continually improving through life's challenges is the cornerstone of what a life should be about.

We accept change and challenges as the landscape we play in. We have developed the habit of learning, and we have a system in place when life brings its best and worst.

This is how the universe and nature work. They are in a constant state of creation and growth and have to adapt to new environments all the time.

If you are not creating your life, the odds will become very hard to recreate when you lose your job or retire. When the flow of life stops, this is stagnation.

If we follow nature, this is just the law of life.
What isn't growing is dying.

The people I follow all have the same rules for life, do what you love, create and grow life, keep doing that until your last breath on earth. It's that simple. Peter Diamandis, Warren Buffet, Charlie Munger, Bill Gates, Dan Sullivan, Richard Branson, and many more follow these fundamental rules about life. If you are not growing and creating your life, you are dying inside life. "It's that simple it's that scary."

Life is either creation or stagnation, growth or death, living or dying, forward or backward, left or right, up or down two sides of the same coin of life. We hold all the cards of life in our hands, and we get to decide which game we would like to play.

Maintaining a life is a safe path to take in life, yet it should not be the path to take if you want to experience life. To experience life, we need to create life and then grow this creation, which ultimately is you. This is the recipe for a life with a creation mindset.

Creation is the process of life; it is in every facet of life.

The universe is in creation, nature is in creation, our bodies are in creation, and so should life. Why do we think we are any different than all the creations that have taken place before us? Creation opens the doors of life, and dying closes the doors of life.

When we apply **The Habit of Creation** to life we are opening up the channels to grow life. The creation process forces you to always move forward in the hatching of new ideas to the creation of yourself. As you create you create a new version of you in the process.

We were put on this earth to become creators. Imagine almost eight billion people in creation and cooperation. What do you think would happen to our world?

The grand challenges we still face today could be eliminated so quickly as a unified force for change. Every single life would be a treasure for the common good of the world.

You are the ultimate creation!

CHOICE

Everything in life comes down to a **choice**. No need to candy coat this, it is what it is. **Simply a choice.**

You're here at this exact moment because of all the choices you have made, and I am here because of all the choices I have made and somehow have brought us together on this cosmic planet we call earth. All this took place because of our choices in life!

Good, bad right wrong backward sideways, the choices are endless and relentless, and they never stop unless you are frozen in ice, yet I'm sure that could be classified as a choice somewhere along the path. So, in theory, if we have unlimited choices, we better be good at making decisions on these choices and figure out a direction for all these choices.

Your choices lead the direction of your life!

Yes, a direction is a plan of where all these choices are heading. Choices are great, choices bring freedom, choices can lead to happiness, and joy bliss hold on. I'm getting ahead of myself here. Yes, and they can also lead to misery. Choices can make your life a living hell if you continue to make the wrong choices in life.

No one can make all the right choices that is impossible, yet we can decide our choices based on the direction we want these choices and our life to head towards.

I am writing this book from my house in Thailand because of one choice I made ten years ago. Yes, one choice that has changed the trajectory of my life forever and a day.

That is how powerful choices can be when we have a direction for our choices. At the time, I didn't realize the direction for my choices, but now it is easy to see. Deep inside, I was looking for a change in a new direction for my life, and it showed up in the form of my wife.

The wonderful thing about life is we all have choices, and these choices will ultimately determine the life we live. We can choose to eat grilled cheese sandwiches every day for the rest of our life, yet would that be a great choice in the end. Tastes great going down but not too good for the rest of the body, no offense to the cheese, the bread, the butter, the grilling, the bacon if you stuff that inside or the tomato soup you dip your grilled cheese into for the mastery of the sandwich.

Every day your body would be screaming at you to give me more of those grilled (thing a me bobs) (Grilled Cheese) because the short term fix is far greater at that moment than the long term effects.

The one thing about life is the actions and choices you make today can have life-altering changes in the future. Short term gain as in the cravings long term pain as in your health. No offense to the grilled cheese sandwich because I ate my share of them in my younger years.

Life is the ultimate game we participate in every day with many options at our disposal every second of our existence. It's mind-numbing if you start to break it down, there is an unlimited amount of decisions and choices. These choices eventually turn out to become the direction of life.

You can read a hundred books from your favorite Guru about the right choice for life, sit on Youtube for a lifetime of videos and never really have any clue as to what the right choices in life should be for you.

The problem with listening to most of these people is that they never get to the root or the foundation of where your growth should start. It's like buying a new car, and the only maintenance you do is wash the car and forget you have to maintain the vehicle.

It's the same as life everyone is walking around inside their life, yet very few people ever get to design their life. When you design your life, you are free to make your life choices, which are not dictated by outside influences.

A choice is making a decision and moving on with that choice. Whether it is the right choice or not, you will never know the choice you didn't make because you can only live the choice you made.

I stopped a long ago trying to over-analyze everything in my life. When I make decisions and choices now, they are at lightning speed because I don't want to weigh down my life worrying if I made the right choice or not.

I know where I'm going, so just that definition alone makes it easier to make decisions for the future. I already have a destination for my life, which is the end of my life.

What does that mean? It means you have the choice in which way your life travels forward or backward, live in creation or stagnation, growing life, or dying inside life. When you stop and think about this reality, it becomes the difference in the way people live and the choices they make for their life.

Grow your life!
Choice

Grow your life, don't stop growing your life until your last breath on earth, and then add one more breath. That is how crucial growing life should be. I added one more breath because that is how vital growing your life should be. I could add a third one. I think you get the point.

You become the creator of your growth, which all comes down to one thing, and that is choice. When you choose to grow your life, it is not in one area of life it is in all areas of life. You adopt a culture and mindset that is rooted in growth at every level of life.

This does not mean you have to be the best, it means you are putting your life's attention on growth and moving forward with your actions. Like anything in life, if a choice is appropriately rooted, there is no sitting back and watching life go by you become an active participant in your life.

You can decide to watch tv every night, or you can decide to read, learn, or workout. You can choose to walk through nature and all its purities, or you can decide to go to the mall in all its enticements. You can choose to meditate and learn what it does for your mind and body, or you can choose to live in stress.

Each activity, when you break it down to the core, is simply a choice. No need to further dissect it apart; it is merely a choice you make for your life.

Now I can go on for thirty thousand words about why growth should be the only choice a life should make, yet I would just be another voice amongst many voices competing for your attention.

You have one life, and your choices will determine the direction of your life. Life only travels in one direction at a time, and we get to choose that direction. We can choose to grow our life, or we can choose to die inside our life.

Die inside Life!
Choice

What does die inside life mean?

You have stopped your forward motion in life, and you are now maintaining a life lived. You are growing old in life as opposed to growing your life.

There is a massive difference when people have a reason for their life vs the people who are maintaining life. One you live with the possibilities that life offers, and the other you live with the accomplishments of a life lived. These, in the end, are choices on how we perceive and live in this world.

I like to listen to people talk because when you hear the words people use to describe life, you can quickly tell if they are **growing** their lives or **maintaining** life. Living in the **past** or growing their **future**. Talking about their **accomplishments in life** or where they are **going in life**. What they **get** out of life vs what they **put** into life. Happy where they **are in life** or how they **can improve in life**.

Your life's direction is based on the reality of a choice to grow or a choice to die. That might sound pretty harsh in its words, but it is at the very core of our existence.

A choice of growth you are focused on your future moving forward with your thought and your actions. You are traveling in a direction that is opening up the doors of your growth.

When you stop your forward motion, you are now maintaining a life where there is little or no growth, and it is straightforward to become a victim of your circumstances. Your life is traveling in the opposite direction; this is just fundamental physics at work here.

Questions and Choice

What are the questions you ask yourself?
What questions do you ask other people?

Do they open up curiosity, intrigue hope, or leave you or the person you ask powerless, speechless, and limited with little or no response. An example of this would be, **Did you talk** with anyone exciting today? Or **What was** the most interesting conversation you had today?

These are choices on how we ask questions. The **did** question left it open-ended with a classic yes or no, and maybe they will elaborate. The **was** question left it for the person to expand their thinking and have a response.

The questions you ask are what you will receive back can dramatically affect the way you live your life. Questions like anything in life can be the gateways for you to experience a richer life. By asking the right types of questions, you can quickly tell a lot about the people you are talking with.

If you want a life that is growing, you ask engaging questions that open up your life. If the other person is engaging and feels the need to reciprocate, you are now playing ping pong with your questions and answers and hopefully having a new experience.

If the question you ask is hollow with no substance, then most certainly the answer coming back will be as well. What you put into life is what you get back, and the questions in life are no different.

- Does it look like it's going to rain today? Yes or no
- How many more rainy days are we going to have of this rain? I don't know, maybe two.
- If I were a duck, all this rain would make me pretty happy, what do you think? This question at least opens up the possibility of an interesting conversation, or they might look at you kind of strange.

A simple choice in life is when we ask the right questions, turning life from dying to growing. One question can open up the doors to learn, grow, and become engaged in life. No questions, leave your doors for growth closed like a refrigerator. You only open the fridge door when you want to put something in or take something out.

Doors are meant to be opened and left open so life can

walk-in, or you can walk out to a new experience.

When we monitor the types of questions inside our lives, we start to control our human experience on earth. We always have to be aware of the questions inside us. We want to have choices in life. The more empowering the questions we ask inside life, the more power we give ourselves in life.

I like to use the universe and nature as my direction and choice to view my existence in life. The Universe has traveled in one direction for the last 14.5 billion years, which is going forward. Nature is continually growing and in creation all around us, and when that growth stops, it starts to die. If it doesn't recreate itself into a better version of itself over time, it becomes extinct.

Everything we need to know about how we should operate our lives is right there. It's not very complicated. We can grow our existence, or we can die inside it. We can let the outside world dictate our life, or we can be our own master of life. We can follow the laws of the universe and nature as our guides and teacher, or we can decide to head in another direction.

At the quantum level of life, we are all made of the same stuff as everything else in the universe and nature. So when we pick a path to choose for our existence, it would make sense to choose the path of least resistance and move in the direction of creation and growth of life.

To summarize **choice** with **Grow or Die,** we need to be like a dancer inside our life. When the music starts, we have a choice in how we interpret the music.

We can let the music grow inside us and then choose how we move through life. We can choose to become a new creation in the dance of life. We can also choose to let the music die inside us without a reaction. We then become a wallflower in the dance of life.

Which life will you choose a life that is growing or one that is dying?

When we apply **The habit of Choice** to life you start to realize that life is a series of choices and each choice can change the direction of your life.

This is something we celebrate in life that we have the opportunity to make choices for our life. To lose that privilege is to lose control of life.

If we choose to grow life we grow.
if we chose to maintain life we begin the slow process
of dying inside life.

MINDSET

**Mindset is something we are born with, or
is it something we can grow?**

A Mindset is the basis for all that you become in life; it will shape your world. A mindset is a belief, how we think, and ultimately becomes the direction for life. It sets the stage for how you perceive the world, the challenges you face, or whether you see the possibilities that life offers or you just want to maintain the status quo.

Do you live with freedom of what life offers, or do your beliefs limit you? A predictable world, or do you live in a world with change and are growing. Do you take things personally, or are you striving to be better? Do you believe certain people are gifted, and there is not much we can do or realize some people are talented yet can also develop those skills with effort and hard work?

When we break down a mindset, it falls into two groups: the growth mindset and the fixed mindset. This is the life's work of Carol Dweck, Ph.D., recognizing the difference between these two groups of people. You are either one of these types, and they both have enormous implications for how you live your life.

You can have two people standing right next to each other experiencing the same event, yet when it comes time to implement or describe the event, they have two different accounts approaches or results to the same event. The difference stems from how their mind works and processes the information, which leads to the difference in mindsets.

So let me ask you a question: Are you the type of person who is always wondering how you are doing in life, or are you the type of person who wonders how you can improve in life? The answer to this simple question will determine the mindset that you have.

Let's dive into the two mindsets and see what we can learn from them both.

Fixed Mindset

- Talent intelligence abilities lie in what they have been given, so there is not much they can do to change in any big way.
- Seeking approval of their intelligence, personality, self-esteem, and character makes them feel good and not look bad in others' eyes.
- Strive for success, avoid failure at all costs, look unintelligent, ignore useful negative feedback, and consider it a personal attack.
- Failure becomes a sign that you were never prepared in the first place, and you were never meant to do that task.
- In relationships, partners or friends lift them continually, making them feel special boost self-esteem.
- They avoid challenges, especially if they can't guarantee they will succeed and feel threatened by others success.
- Covering up weaknesses and showcase strengths.
- Focused on the outcome that becomes their measuring stick for achievement.

Growth Mindset

- Believe talent intelligence is something we develop through effort and hard work it is reserved for the gifted.
- Creates an atmosphere of learning and growing and ac-

cepts criticism as a way to grow forward
- Embrace difficulties and challenges and striving to be better
- Has freedom in thoughts and beliefs and is not held back by limited themselves
- Failures are not setbacks but avenues to grow stronger each time.
- Focus on the process as opposed to the outcome
- Joy in others success

So let's go back to the question again!

Are you the type of person who is always wondering how you are doing in life, or are you the type of person who wonders how you can improve in life?

This question on so many levels is such a great example of both mindsets. In a fixed mindset, they are worried about being judged in a growth mindset, they are more concerned about growing and learning and improving. Fixed mindset when they encounter obstacles they easily give up become disinterested don't challenge themselves to protect their ego.

Growth mindset setbacks are just part of life, a chance to grow and learn to understand the process instead of the results. In short, in a fixed mindset, you are limiting your possibilities in life, and in a growth mindset, you are opening up the possibilities and freedoms that life can have.

There is no right or wrong answer, only observations from two sides of the same coin of life. Whether you are a fixed mindset or a growth mindset, you can slip between the two at different times in your life. The critical point is that individual life situations might require a fixed mindset sometimes than a growth mindset.

To go from a fixed mindset to a growth mindset requires you to think, do, and act in an entirely different manner.

- What are the **words you use** to describe life? The story you tell yourself. You **can** do something vs you **can't** do something. I want to **try and learn,** vs I **don't have** the **ability.** I am **not that good** vs I **can do better.** The words we use in any situation in life have a massive impact on how we live our lives and perceive our world. A growth mindset uses words to grow themselves, whereby a fixed mindset uses words that disempowers them.
- Commit to **learning goals** instead of **performance goals**. You want to be a musician, commit to **practicing every day**. That is how you become a great musician. I was a guitar teacher for ten years, and you could tell pretty quickly the kids who were there to learn how to play guitar because they practiced. The other group were the ones with excuses each week why they didn't have time to practice. When we are continually focusing on **getting better,** that is a growth mindset, and when we are focused on the **outcome, that is a fixed mindset.** If you want to be a great swimmer, the only way to get there is through practice every day. Some people are born with a talent for swimming, yet the next level requires practice, there are no shortcuts. In reality, to always have a growth mindset, it means you are on a never-ending journey, you develop a passion for learning rather than a hunger for approval.
- Suppose you approach **failure as a setback** or devastating a **knock against your ego,** and you continually try to prove to people how great you are. In that case, this is a fixed mindset vs failure in a growth mindset as to what I can learn to get better and **develop a better system going forward.** Also, loss in a growth mindset, you could think you are not fulfilling your true potential. These two differences mean the one mindset you are pointed in the direction of potentials and possibilities

through hard work and learning and the fixed mindset you have failed as a limitation to your abilities.

- Who do you **surround yourself with**? In a fixed mindset, we need people who are continually praising us, picking us up, telling us how great we are, all the things we want to hear. In a growth mindset, we have friends that **challenge us to grow** in life. Look to the people in your immediate group and see how they react to you or other people who follow their chosen words. Are they words to boost your self-esteem, praise you, or choose words forcing you to grow to stimulate your mind?

- **What will it take to go from a fixed mindset to a growth mindset?** This requires you to look to the past and start recognizing patterns present in your everyday life. Why did you choose this type of mindset over another mindset? Becoming aware is the first step along the path. Knowing why you should look at the world through a new set of eyes makes you grow in so many ways. When you start to commit to learning at every level of life, what this does is begin to open up your life to a new way to view the world.

Growth Mindset in our World

Life travels in one direction at a time it can't travel two ways at the same time. This is a choice, and if you want a growing life, having a growth mindset is the only path forward. So what is the ceiling we reach if we are continually achieving more and more with our growth in life?

You soon realize there is always another level if you are willing to stretch, learn, and continue on the process of growth. This is a growth mindset constant and never-ending learning progressing the process. The moment we stop trying and are not pushing ourselves to learn more, do more, act more, and think we have made it in life is the moment we have just fallen into a fixed mindset.

The fixed mindset is easy to slip into at times, yet if we know the signs and want a growing life, we will begin to identify the signs quickly. When challenges arise like life handing you one of its worst, we want a mindset that can thrive in these difficult times, handle the change, and learn and grow. These are the real signs of a life that has adopted a growth mindset.

What is a mindset challenge? This is when you keep expanding and challenging yourself. You became humble and learned to be grateful for all that you have in life. As your mind and life change in dramatic ways, you practice humility and the gift it offers you.

You become curious about life and all that it offers. You open doors windows that are closed because what is on the other side is far more interesting than what you already know and see. You train your mind to keep growing because you are developing a better version of yourself in the process.

You realize the more doors you open, the more opportunity that will present itself. You let the world decide which doors to walk through and which doors to shut. When you train your mind correctly, the only limits we have in our life are the ones we create in our minds.

You are rewarding yourself for all the years of hard and not wasting your time, energy, and your mind on useless and meaningless things that could have robbed you of your true greatness in life. Your focus has been to grow and create life until your last breath on earth.

In the end, this comes down to a choice that you have adopted for your life. The growth mindset vs the fixed mindset. They both have huge implications on the life you experience, the life you live, and the person you become. This is not complicated when we can break it down to our core and start from there.

Life is the ultimate game in the universe, and you start to realize when you are in a growth mindset, you hold all the cards of your life going forward. You are the captain of your ship, the dealer of the cards, and the protector of your life. You know where you are going, which side to live on, and can rise to any occasion in life.

When you grow your life, we have two ways to participate, and they are very different versions of the same event. We cannot get away from the fact that time is ticking, and every second minute hour, day, week, month year that goes by brings us closer to the end of our creation as life here on earth. Yet, we do have a choice on how we interpret how we age.

I hate to use the word age because that usually indicates getting older. When I talk about my life, I typically refer to myself as I am **growing** my life. What this does is change the psychological way I think about myself. I have established that I am continually growing my life, which won't stop until my last breath on earth.

I am growing life vs I am getting older in life. I want to be greater than I was yesterday. I have a future brighter than my past. What do you think the results of a life with this type of mindset will be?

It still comes down to a choice to grow or die inside your life. I don't feel I'm growing my life to die inside it I am growing my life so I can experience more life inside my life.

This completely changes the way you think, act, and become. By changing your mindset, you change the game rules and become the master of your mind and life.

If you portray yourself as getting older, every birthday is a big event, celebrating each year as it is an accomplishment of your life, then you are growing old in life. You become your age.

If you approach life and age as an opportunity to continue to grow life, you move to a different level of life. Getting better the longer you live, having a brighter future than your past, and growing inside life is the anthem song you play for life.

When you apply **The Habit of Mindset** to your life it is the driving force behind your life. It affects everything from healthy relationships and money to abundance wealth and how you perceive yourself in this world.

Your mindset is depicted in your thoughts, words, and actions. A growth mindset is a habit that you will continually grow throughout your life. You look at life as a learning and growing experience in everything you become.

FEEDBACK LOOP

What is a feedback loop, and why should we understand them in our lives?

I n simple terms, it is just information that filters back into our lives to make better decisions as we move on with our life's creation and growth. This is important because we can use this data as a barometer and adjust our actions going forward.

Throughout this book, I will keep coming back to the creation growth concept moving forward with actions. When you have the right information, it is easier to move forward in the direction you want for your life.

In the background of our lives, these feedback loops are running non stop creating our world experience. They are continually receiving information, making assessments of moments, storing this information, then moving forward with actions now or in the future.

Many systems inside our body are run on feedback loops to monitor the conditions and make adjustments to regulate homeostasis inside our bodies. Blood sugar levels, blood pressure temperature, and heart rate are all systems designed around a feedback loop in which they receive information back to make adjustments moving forward.

Everything we do in our lives revolves around some kind of feedback, whether we realize this or not. As soon as we wake up in the morning till the time we go to bed, it is one long feedback of information. Each moment each experience gives us some kind of feedback, and this is information we can use to change the dynamics of life.

In the world of human beings, the way we think, the habits we have, the behaviors we develop, the feelings we store, the emotions we express, and the experiences we have can dramatically change the outcome of our lives.

When we can become aware of anything in our lives and use that information to better our experience, we become the master of life. This would be the real power inside all of us if we chose to develop and use it.

Thoughts create your reality.

- You have a thought
- That thought leads to a choice
- That choice creates an action and behavior.
- That action and behavior produces an experience.
- That experience gets stored in the body as a feeling and emotion.
- That feeling and emotion becomes a memory etched in your mind.

This is feedback of a thought. If this feedback loop were **positive**, you would attach positive emotions to this memory, producing the same feelings. Every time you thought you would produce the same feelings and emotions and have the same experiences. Your body would produce the same chemicals and release them throughout your body, reaffirming your positive feelings.

If the experience were a **negative** one, then the procedure would be the same as the positive feedback loop. Yet, your body would produce and execute a different set of chemicals equal to the negative feelings reaffirming that experience.

The positive and negative feedback loops help establish your personality and identity as they become reflections of you. So it would make sense in the grand scheme of life we started to pay close attention to our thoughts. We could change our life in epic ways.

Let's say we attach a positive emotion to your favorite restaurant, and every time you think of that restaurant, it sends you right back as if you are there experiencing the whole event in your mind. These positive emotions and feelings get attached, producing the same chemicals released into the body to match your feelings. Your body thinks it right there having the experience.

Say you can't stand your co-worker, and every time you see or think of this person, you have negative thoughts and emotions towards them. Then, in reality, you will be producing a chemical rush of feelings and emotions throughout your body, matching these negative feelings. This can happen whether the person is in front of you or you are just thinking of them. To the mind and body, it is all the same.

Do that ten times a day, fifty times a week, one hundred and fifty times a month, or twenty-five hundred times a year; now we have a situation in our lives we must identify as a negative feedback loop.

One emotion, one feedback loop, one moment, now multiply that by the number of negative thoughts and situations you have each day, and this becomes a runaway train of chemicals always rushing throughout your body. This becomes a stressful state for the body.

Our bodies are designed for short term stresses, not long term ongoing events that keep running over and over. When a thought or emotion occurs, it sends the body out of balance. The energy used to maintain the body now has to be used to deal with this event. When the event passes, the energy then can be converted back to help regulate the body.

In negative feedback loops, they are all created inside our

minds as thoughts and expressions of those thoughts. We attach a routine of behavior and actions to an automatic program of re-actions, and now our life runs on autopilot, and we are not even aware of it.

You go to a new coffee house and soon discover the coffee tastes terrible. The service is unfriendly. You leave without finishing your coffee with a bad experience. In this negative feedback loop, chances are you are not going back to this place, so the memory, unless you want to keep talking and remembering the event, will be short-lived inside you.

So what is the difference between the coworker and the coffee place? They are both negative situations creating a negative feel-ing inside your body. You can decide never to go back and relive that experience ending the emotional attachment at the coffee shop.

In the co-worker situation, it is your work and your place of em-ployment, so you can leave and go somewhere else or stick it out and deal with the circumstances. When you leave, the feelings, emotions, and chemical dump in your body **stops**. If you stay, you, your mind, and body have to solve this problem eventually.

I think you have three options.

1. **Stay** - If you stay, then you have to learn to make the changes inside you and change the way you view this person. No longer can you view this person in a hate-fully way, instead in a supportive way. This is hard be-cause you have to make all the changes, yet you will learn to deal with life in the end. Remember, this is your life, not theirs, and when you give into someone else in the form of a reaction, you are giving away your power. If you stay and don't make the changes necessary, you become the victim and the prisoner inside your own life. You have to accept the damage you are inflicting inside your body in the form of stress and stress hor-

mones. No entity on earth can live in a constant state of stress without some form of disease showing up in their lives today or down the road to remind them of their choices in life.

2. **Leave -** If we decide to leave, then all the emotional stress and baggage you have, you can drop it off at the corner and say good riddance and get it out of your life. Life is about choices, and we can decide who or what we want in our life. You find a new job, and hopefully, that new job brings you a positive environment. Even though you left does not guarantee a life free from stress. You have to develop the skill of dealing with people, places, and things that enter your life. Leaving to find another place of employment is adequate for the short term, but eventually, you have to learn to deal with life and the events that show up in many ways. That's life!

3. **Create** The third one would be to create your own life, including your employment. When you work for yourself, you decide what you want in your life designed around you. This is real freedom in life you are responsible for you.

What all three choices do is give you options on a feedback loop. The more information you can assess about life, the more prepared you become moving forward. Whether it is a positive feedback loop or a negative one, we can decide how we go on with our life.

Unknowns

The unknowns in life seem like a scary place. How will you ever predict your future? That is the point you can't, and that is the reason why you should live there at some point in life to feel the unknowns.

The world of the unpredictable is the ultimate feedback loop of life. You soon discover what works and what doesn't in business, relationships, health, where you live, and so much more. When you take that ultimate leap straight into the middle of the unknown, you soon learn a hell of a lot about yourself and life.

We often get trapped and wrapped up inside our lives in this predictable world we call life and lose sight that we live by a program that we have designed. Every day we do the same thing day in and day out. We see the same people, drive the same routes to and from, wake up at the same time, and the list goes on and on.

The problem with this lifestyle is it is very predictable. You become predictable, and when that happens, you become a program that is running your life. The knowns in life are where you live and feel safe, so the chances of ever throwing down the gauntlet and moving to Italy for a year would be nonexistent. One year in Italy, how do you think your life would change, not over the year, but the course of a lifetime.

These events change you forever when you open up the possibilities of what a life can be. The feedback they supply into your life with new experiences is why you need to do something outside your comfort zone.

You could be a very conservative person in one area of your life, but you could be precisely the opposite when it gets to another. You could have a job very secure and never stretch yourself past your point of discomfort because you are insecure about your abilities. The weekend comes, and your interests turn into extreme sports. Now you live in the unknowns where every jump, bend, or hill becomes an adventure. On one side, you are conservative, and on the other, you live on the edge.

Imagine switching on one area of life, your job, and going to live as you go to extreme sports where you live, opening your future doors. With a proper feedback loop in place, you then become the designer of your life.

The only way you ever get to create the life you desire and the future you envision is to create it yourself, and that is not from the knowns in life it is always from the unknowns in life. If you can predict it, then you are living in your past.

When we dissect life to the core, the unknowns in life are how we grow our lives. It is where we go to discover new things, meet new people, invent, create, experience life, visit new countries, and bungee jump. If we don't stretch ourselves that little farther, these moments are lost forever.

Think of your own life when you were in an unknown moment, and you went for it. How did it make you feel, or better yet, how did it change your life? That person you went up to talk to or that country you decided to move to or the food you never tried.

This is very critical when we want to grow a life vs. dying inside our life. To grow anything, it will never be a straight line we need to use our feedback in life to judge how we proceed. Growing at the core should be an opening of life, a birth of an idea, the hatching of creation. This can only take place in the unknowns.

The unknowns are where people go to find their dreams and desires.

Vision

A vision is why you are doing something and not what you are doing.

My Vision for my life is to live to 120 years of age in perfect health and mind and teach people about my experience along the way.

As I write this, not too many people have gotten to the ripe old age of 120 in perfect mind and health. I do have some pluses on my side. I am continually learning and using that information as feedback as to how I grow my life. Yes, I am not getting older in life; I am growing my life.

The way you talk to yourself inside your mind has enormous impacts on your life. Growing is growing. I am moving towards a vision, and aging is dying towards an inevitable outcome. **Which one will you choose?**

I realize I have to be creating and growing my whole life and master my mind and health. Technology is advancing so fast that I might be able to intercept the moment we might get to live to 150 200 years and beyond.

I have many working parts inside this vision of mine moving at different speeds from business relationships, education, investing, creating, and so much more all pointed towards my vision. My life is not about slowing down or aging or a predetermined stop; it is about growing.

I always have a future that is brighter than my past. Using the input, I get from all these various ventures to keep my life moving forwards. I have all the elements working for me simultaneously, not to lose focus on my ultimate goal.

This is my vision for my life. What is yours? When you set up a vision for your life, it explains why you get out of bed each day. You're not just getting up to pay the bills, go to work, do the same thing; you have a bigger purpose for your life. You can be motivated to the moon, yet the real power is a big enough reason why, which is found in your vision.

Success and Failure

Success or failure is just feedback and can tell us a lot about ourselves and how we process each of these events in our life. You need to experience both because it gives a better understanding of where you need to improve in life. There are just events and outcomes on the same coin of life.

Whether you become successful or experience failure, there

is always room to improve. To one person, success could mean something different to the person next to you. Failure is the accurate indicator of a life because this is how you measure yourself, not when everything is going great when it is falling apart.

Success lets face it when you succeed at something, it sends a positive message through your whole body and mind. You can't help but feel good, but this is only the first step. The real success of really successful people is what do they do after this point. Do they push themselves to the next level, or do they become complacent and bask in their glory.

If you have a growing life, there is no such thing as success it's the journey you are on because if you got there, then what's next. Truly successful people have a growing life, and success along this journey is just part of the ride.

Like anything in life, if you are not growing, then you have to be dying. If you have spent your entire life growing this creation that is you in all these areas of your life, why would you ever stop?

When we experience failure, this is the real measuring stick for a human being. Most people look at failure negatively because they take it personally like this is a bad thing. No person on the planet can experience success in everything they do, and if they did, they must not be stretching themselves to any degree in life.

Failure gives you feedback on something you have done or are doing, and you need to improve upon your actions. This is not a negative; it is a readjustment going forward. The people who figure out life's success and failure are the same thing, can go ahead, pick themselves up, and carry on; this is where life's success is.

"Success is when you go up the ladder of life or down it, you are successful at both"

This is the accurate barometer for a life being great when times are great and being great when times fall off a cliff. Then it becomes an exercise between the two as you slowly drift between the two. All great people in history will tell you it's the failures of the setbacks in life, which made them not the successes.

Oprah Winfrey, Nelson Mandella, Victor Frankl all overcame horrible circumstances and failures in their lives to become very successful in life. As each failure or setback knocked them back, they used their feedback in their lives to make them stronger after each incident. Finally, when they broke free, they all excelled in their lives; these people are inspirations of life.

The feedback loop is essential, especially when we can use this information to make ourselves stronger as we go forward in life.

If you have a growing life, then this feedback is essential to grow your life. If life is on autopilot and just maintaining life, this information only becomes philosophy and wisdom. Utilizing the tools you have at your feet can make your life a masterpiece.

When we apply **The Habit of Feedback Loop** to our lives, we begin to realize that everything we do becomes a feedback loop for the next event. How we process, this information will be the difference in how we live life.

When we become aware of this constant data that is life, and we are directing ourselves according to the path we have chosen, we are moving in the direction of our lives.

ENVIRONMENT

**Create an environment where you can grow instead
of an environment where things go to die!**

This opening statement is a powerful realization because you ultimately decide the environment you want to grow life inside. When you are growing, you are opening the doors of life, and when you are dying, you are closing the doors of life. What environment sounds like the ideal place to grow life?

When you are growing, your environment will be in constant change, which becomes a byproduct of growth. The more doors you open, the more change that will occur. So you will have to be very good at accepting, adapting, and moving forward with action to thrive in the river of change and grow a life.

In a growing environment, you are creating and adapting to the changes that are happening, and once you get used to the constant change, it becomes an environment in which you thrive. Change represents growth, which alters your environment.

Accept, adapt, move forward with action, and these become the three laws that you operate your life by. This is when you go from student to master of your life and ultimately master yourself, where all the power in life resides.

When life happens, the good, the bad, or the ugly, you are always in control of every step of the process. You accept the new reality, adapt to your new environment, and move forward with your actions.

This formula guarantees you will never get overwhelmed when

life hands you one of those moments that alters your life and changes your environment. You have been practicing for these moments your entire life with your own life.

The Comfort Zone
Environment

What makes you comfortable in life makes you soft and can ruin your life, yet what is uncomfortable will grow your life!

Nothing about a comfort zone inspires greatness in life, yet so many people want to feel safe and harbor inside the zone of comfort. The real growth of any life is in the unknown and not the known.

A comfort zone is strictly inside our minds as this imaginary environment we have decided is real. The dimensions become our limiting beliefs, a mindset that has been established and accepted as the boundaries for life. It is a risk-free environment free from growth and change.

How did they get established, and why? Who taught you this way of thinking? When we are born, we are free from limitations, yet as we get older, we start to develop limitations over time, and these become the restrictions we put onto our lives.

The problem with a comfort zone is that it gets comfortable to be comfortably trapped inside your environment, and you lose the ability to stretch yourself into what you were meant to be!

Imagine a life that has all the opportunity in the world to grow, expand, learn, master one's self, and be the actual creator of life. Eventually growing into who you were meant to be. This is an exciting life full of potential and possibility.

Imagine a world that lives to play it safe inside a make-believe world where the rules established are all inside the mind—disempowered from the potentials and possibilities that life could have experienced.

The reason for this way of life is because.......?
The reason you can't expand your life is because.....?
The reason I have these rules for my life is because....?
The reason I live in this comfort zone is because.......?

We can come up with a million reasons why we do anything in life. Living in a zone where we don't challenge ourselves to be greater is not a recipe for growth.

I like the simple approach to life when I question life and what I should do, I simply walk out my front door, look up into the night sky, and observe. The universe is expanding, creating, and growing right before my eyes. So this is a good indication of what I should be doing for my life and inside my environment.

When you want to discover who you are and what you are made of eventually, you have to open that door, climb over that wall and expand past the perimeter. Once you take your first steps past any imaginary line in the sand, you have just expanded, and it is hard to go back to where you came.

This can be a voluntary movement as testing your comfort zone limits, which is excellent for establishing a larger zone. In most cases, we are forced outside of our zone by the outside world. This can show up in life's disguise as life-altering moments, events, happenings, stress, and many more discomforts.

We have no choice but to expand past our zone's borders at this point as we adjust to a new environment. We can make changes in times of distress or make changes free from the stress of happenings and learn to grow past our limiting beliefs.

In the end, this comes down to a choice in life. We are all held up to some degree inside our imaginary walls that we have established. The environment stays the same if we don't push on the walls for growth.

Some people grow immense comfort zones expanding at a fast pass, in this case, their environment is in a constant state of change and growth. They are in alignment with the universe.

In a dying environment, the doors of life are shut there is little movement in terms of change, and your life becomes very predictable. Take the last five years and place them in front of you, and your past now becomes your future.

It is a safe environment in terms of change until you are forced to change, then you have no choice to grow. Every person, place, or thing brings you back to your familiar, safe zone.

The pain of change becomes overwhelming, having to adjust to a new environment. So you end up seeing the same people do the same things and relive the same experiences over and over.

You could hate your job, despise your boss, have nightmares over your co-worker, agonize over your drive to and from work, stay in a relationship just for convenience, live in a city you can't stand, stress over financials, all because you don't like change.

To change is more painful than the present reality of what you relive at every moment. Becoming safe in your environment, thinking, is not the approach to long term health.

Every minute, hour, day, week, year that goes by, you have the same chemical cocktail rush of feelings, emotions, stress coursing through your body, reaffirming your addiction to each person, place, or thing you have in your life. All this is happening throughout your body on autopilot without an end in sight.

There is only one conclusion to this scenario, and it comes in the form of illness and disease just because you hate change. Your environment will most certainly change at this point to a new reality.

The **World Health Organization** (WHO) calls it Lifestyle choices as the health epidemic of nations everywhere in the twenty-First century. Heart disease, cancer, and autoimmune disease now account for 85% of today's illnesses and deaths in wealthy countries and rising.

Lifestyle choices become the environment we continually live in and accept as our reality for our life. So how do you change when all of your life you have been programmed to live and exist in a certain way?

You have to become greater than the environment you continually accept as your world. You have to grow past all your limiting beliefs about growth change and the environment and believe there is a better world out there on the other side.

When you are in a constant state of change, that is where the growth of any life exists. When you become uncomfortable, that is a sign and a chance to experience a new degree of life. There is always another path if you are willing to go down that road.

To grow a garden of life, you need soil, water, sunshine, and mother nature to do her thing. The garden of life in the right environment can grow in most places. In varying degrees, all these ingredients come together to form the basis for a solid footing to grow life.

We ultimately choose what we plant in our garden and what takes root and grows. Do we want color for the eyes, smell for the nose, feel for the touch, or taste for our pallet? At times we will also need to pull out the weeds to keep our environment healthy.

Your environment has two realities, the one inside you and the one outside you. This becomes a balancing act and how we process these two worlds.

You could have twin boys who react in two different ways yet live in the same environment. They could have an alcoholic father, and one twin says he drinks because my father is an alcoholic, and the other twin says I don't drink because my father is an alcoholic.

The same environment yet two different scenarios they have processed. This is an excellent example of two different environments.

Today as I am writing this, the world is in the depths of the coronavirus Covid 19, and this is an excellent example of the environment and the two worlds.

The coronavirus doesn't know borders or human beings; it is a virus looking for a host environment to grow. Just like the flu or any other virus, it wants to grow and live and survive. The last thing it wants to do is kill the very environment it is now occupying because that means it dies as well.

Governments worldwide closed their borders, restricted air travel, canceled gatherings, closed businesses, and stopped people's movement. Told their citizens to social distance, wear masks, and stay indoors in an event to control the virus.

Controlling the environment outside us is a great start. What about the environment inside us that protects us from colds, viruses, flu, bacteria, and toxins we experience every day? What are we doing to make that environment as healthy as possible?

A healthy immune system is our best defense against any virus. That is an environment that you do have control over. Yet to tell your citizens to eat healthy, stop drinking, eliminate stress, practice deep breathing exercises to develop a stronger immune system might not be that popular.

The first step I took was to look to the people I thought would give me the truth about what I should do. I learned quickly from multiple sources that a healthy immune system was your best defense against the virus.

I installed the systems in my life quickly to better strengthen my immune system. I also learned what weakened the immune system and eliminated them from my life.

When you want to gain access to your life strengths, you work with what you have in life and move on. If you are making changes in your life and changing your environment, you can react quickly and adjust to the changes.

When events happen outside of you, like a health issue, job loss winning the lottery, or anything that changes your life outside you, you can adjust accordingly to further your life journey.

I like to think that everyone on the planet is their own universe. We get to stand every day in the middle and make the choices that will move our life forward.

When you do this, you have created real power in your life. Not a power over others, a power over yourself.

I create moments for my life where I am one with myself and the environment I have created. It comes in the form of meditation practice I have adopted for my inner self. When you become still and breathe in the present moment, you are one with everything inside you and around you.

When you spend time free from distraction inside an environment you have created, you can gain access to a new level of life. When life happens, you are ready for whatever the world has in store for you.

Birds can fly anywhere in the world, yet most birds stay close to home, the environment they are used to. A goldfish in a fishbowl will only grow to the fish bowl's size, yet put that goldfish into a pond, and he begins to grow in size as he adjusts to his new environment.

We all have choices in our lives. We can be birds with an **opportunity** to go anywhere with our lives, yet we chose to play it safe and never experience the world beyond us. When given the opportunity, we can be a goldfish that will continue to grow larger, not held back by the limitations of space or the mind.

What will you choose for your environment?

Your environment is the playground for life. When you're a kid running around, you just play, there are no boundaries, only fun. Everything was new, exciting, fresh, and every minute was a new experience. You just lived in your little world of make-believe, where anything is possible.

As we get older, we lose that ability to live in that make believe world where everything is possible. Instead, we start to erect the walls of our life around our real-life experiences and the ones we have developed in our minds.

We become birds
sitting on a branch watching the
world go by

When we apply **The Habit of the Environment,** we see where we've come from, where we are right now, and where we are going. If they all look the same, then the environment hasn't changed at all. If you only know one environment, how will you ever know what is on the other side?

The other side is where we go to grow life. That environment might be a new experience that sends your life in a new direction!

EVOLUTION

**Evolution is a never-ending process of growth creation
and expansion until it starts dying!**

T oday scientists have figured out that the universe is expanding at an alarming rate of roughly seventy km every second. That is faster than the speed of light. Edwin Hubble in the 1920s discovered that the nearest galaxies to our milky way were receding from our galaxy. The farther away they are, the faster they are receding.

The universe is in a constant state of creation, growth, and expansion and has been for 14.5 billion years. It is hard to get a grasp on the magnitude of its sheer size when we're standing on our tiny planet Earth tucked away inside the milky way.

The milky way galaxy is one of billions of galaxies that exist in the universe. There are approximately one hundred billion stars in each galaxy, with a planet revolving around each star. So technically, there could be thousands if not millions of solar systems just like ours just inside the milky way galaxy. It is staggering even to comprehend.

**The only thing we can do is be great observers
and follow in this giant's footsteps.**

The Universe is in the creation and growth phase of its existence and shows no signs of stopping; if anything seems accelerating. Eventually, like a balloon, it will hit its maximum size and halt its expansion and precipitate its ultimate demise. This will be a fun time. I don't think we want to be around for this event, just thinking.

Inside the universe, that's where all the chaos lives. This is an organized chaos because when you observe it closely, you find that everything like galaxies, solar systems, stars, planets, and so much more are all creating and growing constantly. When they stop this phase, they eventually die.

When we take this one step further, we see the same evolution is taking place everywhere on our planet. When something stops growing, it starts to die, and if it can't change with the times and evolve into a better version of itself, it becomes extinct. To be blind to this fact, we become poor observers of what is going on in nature and our universe.

Even the majestic rocky mountains evolved over time. Eighty million to fifty-five million years ago, many plates began sliding under the North American plate. Much tectonic activity and erosion from glaciers have sculpted them throughout the years. Today they experience change and eroding, yet these changes take place over millions of years.

When we observe nature and all its entities, they seamlessly understand their existence on the planet. They all live in co-operation because nothing exists just to exist. If the hungry lion wants to eat, he eats. He doesn't go out and kill ten zebras, he kills one. Bees pollinate, helping flowers grow, a bird flies, a fish swims, ants march, grass grows, and the life cycle keeps going.

They all have a purpose, a meaning, and when they stop growing, they die. If they can't evolve, they become extinct. It's that simple, and it's been happening for millions and millions of years.

We, Homo Sapiens, have kind of missed the message that the rest of nature and the universe understand so well. We don't live in harmony and co-operation with our surroundings. We try to dominate and end up being in constant conflict with our environment.

We have compartmentalized our life with borders, walls, governments, religion, race, society, and everything to separate ourselves from the very existence of life.

Is this why we were put on this earth to divide like an equation?

When we closely examine our outer world, which is in a constant conflict, and our inner world, which is the fifty trillion cells that keep us alive, they tell two different stories.

The fifty trillion cells are a community all working together for the well being of their host. They all have a job to do, and they pass information around to each other at the quantum level. Their goal is to sustain life.

When a cell has lived its life and dies, another cell is there to take its place. It is a beautiful living organization where fifty trillion cells all work and communicate instantaneously in complete harmony. The human body is a petri-dish for the fifty million cells that keep it alive.

When cells in a body start to go against each other or fight each other, diseases like cancer, heart disease, and autoimmune disease begin to take hold. The very word autoimmune disease means self-destruction. A body has been living out of harmony with the universe.

We don't want to die too long and live too short.

When we view our world today, things are breaking down, and they are becoming unsustainable. The way of life we have been used to living, which is based around competition to divide and conquer only the fittest survive corporate structures, is starting to fall apart. This is based on Darwinian thinking. Charles Darwin released his book the Origin of Species by means of natural selection in the mid-1800s.

We have to look no further than climate change as a prime example of this way of thinking. How long do we last as a planet when we continuously put profit ahead of common sense. We build our whole existence on this planet around a resource that we burn that poisons the atmosphere. At the time, it made sense because of the industrial revolution, yet 130 years later, we are still reliant.

Scientists can develop a million research papers and reasons why climate change over time will correct itself, yet they have missed the point. The truth becomes, is this a sustainable way of life for our existence on the planet?

If you asked any grade, one student, they would know the correct answer. Their minds are clear and not distorted and talk from their heart and not from their heads. Instead, we spend millions and millions on research papers and fancy graphs to try to justify our reliance.

Billions and billions of dollars spent trying to implement changes to a society that has yet to buy into the fact that change is inevitable. If we don't change, we die. We pay the price today, or we pay the price tomorrow with extinction. That could be twenty years from now, one hundred 200 or longer, just a blip in the cosmic timetable.

In the grand scheme of the universe, if we were to go extinct, would it matter? What makes us so unique? In our world, we are special, yet to the universe, what does it mean? Maybe the universe is playing a game with us to see how long we last before we can figure ourselves out or blow ourselves up.

If we worked in harmony with the universe and mother nature, we would be using the sun's energy as our source and growing our existence. The sun is a nuclear reactor in the sky and holds our whole solar system together and doesn't take days off.

Most entities on the planet use the sun's energy to grow and create their existence. Why would we think we can be so different from them when most entities have been on the planet for millions and millions of years. They have a lot to teach us about survival.

Remember, If we are not a growing planet, then we become a dying planet. If we are not growing as Homo Sapiens, then we must be dying as Homo Sapiens. Our existence can only travel in one direction at a time.

This is just paying attention to our environment and what nature shows us every day and using that to fuel our future. Self-empowerment being in control of our lives and creating ourselves at every level and then working in cooperation with everything around us.

There are signs now that a consciousness is starting to build where people are now beginning to wake up because we have to do something. There are companies leading the way for bettering the planet like Tesla, Toms Shoes, Patagonia, Beyond Meat, Body shop, and so many more. Well Established companies like Ikea and Walmart have started to change to become more environmentally friendly.

This is an evolutionary time and what that means is the old paradigm that we have been living is starting to fall apart. Our old way of thinking is beginning to change. This is a good sign because a new one is being created, yet with change will come pain as we shift between the two different ideologies.

If there is no pain, then we haven't collectively accepted that we need to change.

We have to embrace change in a healthy way and go from an unsustainability model to a world of sustainability where we all work together as one. Our old way of thinking has to make way for a new level of thought free from alternative motives. We need a new story for our world going forward.

Human behavior will be difficult to change as we are so divided in our worlds. It is hard to solve the problems with the same brain that created the problems in the first place, so we need the next generation to step up to be the voice of change. It will be their world in the future, not ours.

A new way of life, thinking, and actions is based on cooperation in society. The evolution is people coming together and creating, growing, and sharing for the common good of their community, large or small, and for the world.

This is the path that we need to turn to because that is how we can sustain our growth through cooperation, not competition. Nature and all the entities that call earth home just live their existence so effortlessly. They get it, and we need to find it. They live it, we need to breathe it. They have been evolving, and we are just revolving.

We have the most complex brains on the planet, so it would make sense we used our collective consciousness to grow into the world we were meant to live in. Surely we can figure this one out in time to help grow this magnificent jewel we call earth.

Growing or dying in the end,

it just becomes a choice!

When we apply **The Habit of Evolution** it starts with you first ask yourself truthfully is your world evolving or revolving. Are you working with mother nature or against. Is the life you are living sustainable for the next two hundred years? Are you looking at making changes that will help the evolution of our planet for the future?

Your next car have you thought about purchasing an EV? Do you recycle as much as possible? How about a solar roof for your house? These are just a few questions we can now ask ourselves to better shape our world for the future.

If we want to leave the planet in better shape than when we were born the conversations and decisions have to start now. We only have one world.

HEALTH

You are the owner of your health!

When you own anything, you will do everything you can to look after it. That new car, your schooling, a new toy spaceship, the house you moved into, or that fabulous new rice cooker you've had your eye on. If you want it bad enough and desire to own it, you can always get it.

These are all great things to own, yet they all represent things outside us. The relationship, at some point, has to come to an end. The ownership changes hands, vanishes into thin air or goes into the recycling bin for its next creation. We become vessels as we pass around life's objects of ownership.

The **timeframe** for each item is different. The level of **commitment** to that item varies drastically. The value we **associate** usually starts to ween overtime. There is always the **next** thing to come along that is better than what we currently have. For everyone, the timeframe, commitment, and association are different, yet that makes us human.

There are 300,000 items in the average home in America, and ten percent of these items are held off-site in storage facilities. That is a lot of ownership of stuff you eventually have to say goodbye to. Every item layers a sense of time and responsibility in this relationship. You need it, buy it, use it, and get rid of it— the life cycle of things you own.

A car is a classic example of ownership. Almost every car you purchase goes down in value. The more you drive, the more money it costs in gas, repairs, and insurance. The longer you own, the more it depreciates until one day, if you own it long enough, your paying just to get rid of it, or the car outlives you.

A car makes you feel good as it should, drives you around to get you where you're going, yet one day the relationship will end.

In most people's worlds, the more stuff they own, the harder they have to work. Ownership has its privileges and also its setbacks. In the big picture of life, these are just things. They are great too own at the time and what they represent to you but don't mean much at the end of your life. You cant take them with you.

Your Health

Your health is ownership and stays beside you your entire life. You couldn't get rid of it if you tried. It starts at birth in your mother's womb and ends with your final breath. In between is called life, and how we process this world over our lifetime will determine how we feel grow age and who we finally become.

Your health is you. It is not outside you it is inside you it's personal. To explain your health to someone else is impossible because they are not you. What you feel could be entirely different from the person sitting next to you. They could be climbing mountains and have the energy of the world inside them, and you're having a hard time climbing out of bed with zero energy to make it through the day.

Health is a labyrinth of many life factors, yet the first place you have to start is in your mind. Say the words **I AM HEALTH.** These are powerful words to say to yourself because whenever you use these words, I Am.... you begin a relationship. With health, this is a forever commitment.

I am health as thoughts or words tell your mind and body that you have a direction for your health to follow. You have to be careful how you dialogue with the mind. The immune system is listening all the time to give it words for healing and health, or you can give it words to become ill and sick.

This becomes a choice for any life which way you would like to travel. You're the guard at the gate, so you can choose what you allow into your world. If you can fix your thoughts, you can also fix your health it has to start somewhere.

- words are powerful
- information is powerful
- actions are powerful
- negative thoughts leave you powerless
- negative thinking leaves you powerless
- no action leaves you powerless

If you want a healthy mind and body, you have to become a healthy mind and body. If you want an unhealthy mind and body, you become an unhealthy mind and body. Healthy thoughts lead to healthy choices for healthy actions and then to a healthy body. We are aligning our health so we can get the most out of life.

When we treat symptoms and not where the problem originated we are putting band-aids on to bigger issues for the future

When diet after diet becomes the solution to your weight problem, are you addressing where the problem originates? Symptoms are signs from the body, telling you of a problem that needs to be addressed. This way of thinking starts in the mind first.

When you're sitting in the doctor's office trying to explain how your feeling and you're his tenth patient that day, what do you think it sounds like to him?

Doctors are human they have heard your symptoms a thousand times before. At that split moment, he has to make an educated guess to the problem. Issue tests a prescription or to a specialist. Does he have the whole picture of you in front of him?

You have a choice, be the creator of health or the victim of health. Grow your health or die inside your health. Live by the symptoms of life or get to the core where the problem originates.

The truth is a healthy body fights disease while an unhealthy body is trying to ward off disease. The word disease is derived from the word **(Dis-Ease)**, a body that is not at ease.

People who have great health have a spark a certain frequency about life, and you can see it in their eyes, smile, and in their words. Are they the lucky ones, or have they been working on their health their entire lives? Thousands and thousands of choices over their lifetime?

Ninety-seven percent of babies born today in most developed countries are born healthy. They start in this world pure as snowflakes and begin developing their mind-body and health. This ownership lasts a lifetime, so it would make sense that we look after it, protect it and love it, and cherish it. There is nothing you will own in life that has more effect on you than the ownership of your health it is the catalyst for life.

- Your health is something you own.
- If you want a healthy body, you become a healthy body
- You grow your health by the choices you make every day
- Health care is actively taking part in your health every day
- Sick care is losing control of your health to illness and disease
- Lifestyle choice will dramatically affect your health
- Eighty-Five percent of people today will die from **heart disease, cancer,** or some form of an **autoimmune disease.**
- Most people will never live to their eighty-first birthday

These are just facts of life, and they have a massive influence on the way we grow or die inside life.

> **"The doctor of the future will give no medicine
> but will interest his patients in the care of the human frame
> in diet and in cause and prevention of disease."**
> Thomas Edison 1902

What is so remarkable about this statement from Thomas Edison is that he knew back in 1902 that the road to health was when you take control of your health. This was when the three leading causes of death were **pneumonia, gastrointestinal,** and **tuberculosis.**

In one hundred and twenty years, our entire society has changed the way it is dying. Every day worldwide, **49,000** people die of heart disease, **26,000** from cancer, **4300** from diabetes, **2100** from suicide, **1287** humans killing humans, and the list keeps going. This is every single day these are mind-numbing figures.

So what is happening to our world?

The **World Health Organization** (WHO) calls it lifestyle choices. The choices we decide every day for our life is what's killing people around the world. Everything from diet, stress, exercise, friends, drugs, jobs to the barrage of negative news people immerse themselves into.

We all have the power to choose what we allow into our lives. We hold all the responsibility in our hands.

- Food doesn't choose you - you choose the food you eat
- Stress doesn't choose you - you allow stress into your life
- Exercise doesn't choose you - you chose to go for a walk
- Friends don't choose you - you chose your friends
- Drugs don't choose you - you chose to take drugs
- Job doesn't choose you – you chose your job
- Negativity doesn't choose you - you chose to be negative

What we eat, the stress we live in, the inactivity of our bodies, the friends we choose, the drugs we consume, the job we take, and the negativity we allow into our lives are just the starting points to the decisions we make about our lives.

Everything we do positively or negatively will have huge impacts on our health in the future.

We cause the effects in our life through daily routines and habits. If we take our past and never question, we are not paying attention to our future. When a way of living gets passed down through generations does not mean that it is the way forward for today.

To give you an example, I loved drinking milk growing up; I couldn't drink enough. I also had allergies so bad and had a hard time functioning without heavy doses of medication to get me through a day. One day I was reading a book called Diet for a New America by John Robbins, and that was the day I stopped drinking milk.

Thirty years later, I have never suffered a day of allergies, and my bones are strong and healthy—this an example of cause and effect. Not willing to question and discover the correlation between the two, I would have lived another thirty years of allergies. Also, the untold damage I would have caused inside my body by taking this type of medication.

When people get stuck and are not willing to look at what they are doing, they become victims of their future. Sometimes the solution to a problem is right before your eyes. Question everything to find out if your habits and routines are slowly killing you inside.

Decisions today will eventually be delayed reactions inside our bodies. They show up years later in the form of illness and disease. When we live without awareness, we also have to accept the results that will show up eventually.

Food tastes great, sitting on the couch watching tv feels relaxing, drinking alcohol after a stressful day at work feels rewarding, and taking drugs alters your reality. After years of these activities, are we growing our health? Are these activities positive or negative? What Is the message we are sending to our immune system?

When the mind is in control, we tend to make better decisions for our lives. When the body is in control, we give in to our feelings, cravings, stress, negativity, alcohol, drugs, and that sense of no control. It becomes a downward spiral with no control and one day waking up with a new challenge for life.

We have a choice for our lives
Health Care or Sick Care!

Health care **is you,** and sick care is **outside you**. Health care is about preventing illness and disease, and sick care is about treating illness and disease. Health care is designed around a **healthy lifestyle**, and sick care results from an **unhealthy lifestyle**. Doctors get paid when you are **sick** they don't get paid if you become **healthy**. Proper health care starts in mind first and **costs nothing**, and sick care in the United States, the treatment of illness and disease costs over **3.5 trillion** $ a year.

Countries fill their hospitals up with sick people with no solution in sight. As a patient, you have to realize where you are on the ladder of health. In the case of bypass surgery, patients usually have the procedure repeatedly, does this solve the problem or ignore the inevitable. We spend billions each year fixing the immediate danger, yet should the solution be best addressed at the core where it started

If you don't change your lifestyle, you can't change your life, and It becomes a revolving door. If you don't start with your mindset first, it will be hard to know where to begin to move forward. A life of freedom soon becomes the walls of a prison inside your life.

**"There is a living tapestry of men and women
and the quality of our lives will depend
upon how much each of us is prepared
to take responsibility for ourselves"**
Margret Thatcher

Health Care

My definition of **Health Care** is when you become 100% responsible for your health and actively participate in your growth—becoming aware of all that is happening inside your body physically and mentally. As the body sends out signals and signs, it becomes our job to uncover these messages. You have a long term goal to live in well-being your entire life where the mind and body act as one. You are not interested in solutions that are for the moment that are temporary. This is a lifetime commitment to become aware, educated, and make the necessary changes to live the best possible life you can live.

Example

When you have inflammation, what is your body telling you? Was it something you ate that triggered it, or have you been living this way for years, and now it becomes you as a way of life?

Inflammation is a sign that something is not right in your body. Yes, you can take a prescription to mask the symptoms, yet that is not fixing the problem and, in the long run, only making matters worse.

When I grew up, we all loved eating breads, pastries, pasta, pizza, breakfast cereals, buns, donuts, and most things with wheat and flour. We just ate like everyone else, and the food tasted great. Wheat and flour is everywhere in supermarkets and most fast-food restaurants.

In my mid-thirties, I suffered from inflammation badly, so taking huge doses of Ibuprofen became a way of life. It was something I just lived with, not paying close attention to what was causing it. Taking pills to alleviate the pain was easy, no thought involved. Feel pain take pill rinse and repeat, yet the pain never went away it always returned.

I started to educate myself on the effects that food had on my body. I experimented by eliminating certain foods from my daily diet and feeling its impact on my health.

Then I began adding a healthier food choice again, monitoring the effects. I never realized what I was eating could have such a dramatic effect. When I changed to a plant-based diet, the results were terrific. My inflammation disappeared. I started eating real food vs dead food.

I was willing to make a change in my lifestyle long enough to see the results. When you feel great, why would you ever go back to the old way of eating. When I experience small bouts of inflammation, I've always traced back to something I've changed in my diet or eaten.

To give you another example, I want to live to 120. I want to walk into that birthday with a strong mind-body and health. I want to accomplish this by listening to my mind and body to adjust my actions to get the best optimal health.

My life and my health have a long term plan for their existence. I want balanced health, not unbalanced health. What I mean is I'm in a constant state of listening to the signals my body is sending and then readjusting to get me back to my optimal health.

Whenever I add or subtract anything new into my life, I am always paying attention to the results. As my body and mind are changing, so am I.

You could be spending two hours a night in the gym on advice from well-informed fitness instructors, yet is that what your body is telling you what you need.

You could be taking 75 vitamins a day because some health expert says that you need to stay healthy, yet is that what your body is telling you. If we become blind in our actions and run our lives on autopilot, we will ignore our bodies' signs.

I implemented a daily meditation practice into my life, and this has had dramatic effects. Having experimented with meditation on and off for years, I never practiced it long enough to feel these great results people kept talking about. When I finally committed and made it a daily habit, it has changed how I live and experience my world—one word CLARITY.

When I work, I work. When I create, I create. When I'm with my family, I'm with my family. When I read, I read. I don't live in stress, and when I do feel stress starting to bubble to the surface, I am quick to send it off in another direction.

I'm willing to add something new into my life, assess how it reacts with my body and mind, and see if it has a place in my life for the future. This is how you grow your health by taking the responsibility into your own hands because you know yourself best.

My life is all about healthy choices as I grow and move forward with my life. I have a purpose for my health, designed around moderation, and making sure I can find the perfect balance. This is how I live in Health Care every day, which will last my entire life.

Sick Care

My definition of sick care is when you hand your health over to someone who starts to decide about your health for you. This could come in the form of a Doctor, Physician, Surgeon, Psychiatrist, or whoever can make decisions on your behalf. You could be in treatment for weeks or months in a hospital or be handed prescriptions to recover at home. When you lose your free will in life, it is tough to get it back.

At home, your pharmacist now has to administer the prescriptions check doses potential side effects, and be the conduit between your doctor and you. On the scale of treatment, all these people now have a direct influence on your life.

At one time, you made all the decisions about your life, and now you are at the mercy of someone else who might not have your best interests at heart.

Sick care represents billions and billions of dollars for corporations and trillions of dollars for governments to administer. This is big business and a lot of invested interests.

Pharmaceutical companies invent new drugs to treat the symptoms of illness and disease they are not really in the business to make you well. If everyone got better and didn't need what they were offering, they would be out of business. These are just facts.

Sick care is the treatment of illness and disease

Everyone gets sick from time to time we are only human. A lot is happening in this world beyond our control. It shows up in the form of viruses, germs, bacterial infections, and many more, and if we don't have a strong enough immune system in place, then we need help from the outside world.

So what role do we play when we get heart disease, cancer, or an autoimmune disease? Are they something we are born with, or is it something we develop over time?

When we look at the leading causes of death from 1900 and 2020 as earlier written in this chapter, we see two entirely different stories. How can there be such a huge difference in the way people are dying?

World Health Organization

- **Lifestyle choices** are the reason why people are getting sick today. We can live to seek knowledge, or we can live blind and do nothing it is a choice. Lifestyle choice goes at the heart of most people's lives it becomes personal. If your life is off-balance, there is a reason, and it becomes your opportunity to find out the cause.

- Do you stand on the side that says we are free to make our own choices in life, and no one will tell me how to live my life? So you live not paying attention to the signs your body is sending you.
- **Stress** is the health epidemic of the twenty-first century. Stress is a choice you decide for your life it is not something we are born with. When you chose everything in your life, you can also determine the level of stress you want for your life
- Is stress something you have under control, or does it rule your world? Does it guide your decisions in life with its perception, actions, and reactions?
- Stress is the eight hundred pound gorilla in the room that is always there if left unchecked

No organism can live in a constant state of stress there is a breaking point for everything. Animals can turn on and off the hormones of stress when an event has passed. A zebra gets chased and outruns the lion and is back grazing with the event behind.

Humans beings can turn on and off the stress hormones after events, just like animals. The difference is humans can relive the event over and over in their minds. To the brain, it doesn't know the difference between the actual event or the one that is being played out inside your head. To the brain and mind, it is the same thing.

If you don't control your thoughts, you start playing the event repeatedly in your mind like a recording and reliving the event. The same chemical rush each time is being released throughout your blood system, recreating that feeling. This is the sad truth for millions and millions of people throughout the world.

When you look at stress, this is one event played out ten times a day, three hundred times a month, thirty-six hundred times a year. Then multiply that by the number of other things that stress you out, and now it is a runaway train of life heading to an eventual outcome.

Is this your life or someone you love? Were we put on this planet to live in stress? How much stress is from your own doings about change? Do you believe you have options in life about stress?

These are hard questions to answer, yet they are at the heart of sickness, illness, and disease everywhere around the world. As societies have grown and developed, so have our need for treatment, and it becomes a huge wheel that just keeps spinning and getting bigger all the time.

So what is the solution?

A solution to a problem about health is immense, yet it has to start somewhere, and it has to start in your backyard, and that backyard is you. If most of us are born into this world healthy, and by the time we turn eighty, we are riddled with illness and disease, how much of that responsibility is ours?

We have to wake up and realize that we control our lives no one else does. When we hand our health over to someone else, we lose the ability to make our own choices. Health starts in your mind.

Every time we think, there is a chemical reaction, and the brain produces a chemical. That chemical gets released into the body, and the body reproduces that chemical and sends a message back to the brain matching that chemical. Now the body and the mind are on the same page.

As you think you become. If you think positive thoughts, you become positive thoughts. You are releasing powerful drugs throughout your body naturally; this helps maintain and rejuvenate the body.

If you think negative thoughts, you become negative thoughts. Each thought releases chemicals equal to those thoughts throughout your body, sending your body out of homeostasis, and now your fighting with your health.

Thoughts have got to be at the forefront of most things in our life because that is where everything starts. We are thinking machines, and we can think ourselves in and out of health.

Mindset will determine your beliefs and how you interpret your world. You can change your thoughts in your mind a lot faster than you can change your body.

Knowledge is power, and power is when you start to take life back and make the right decisions growing life forward. One of my life influences has been Dr. Joe Dispenza, who has written three incredible books that have completely changed how I think, do, and act in this world.

These books are must-reads for anyone that wants to live a better and growing life free from the limiting beliefs that hold people back. **Breaking the Habit of Being Yourself, You are the Placebo,** and **Becoming Supernatural.**

Joe's books tackle what is possible for a life, not the limitations of life. Joe breaks it down at the quantum world where everything starts in the first place.

Anytime you can gain a wealth of information that changes the way you think, alters your perception about what is possible, and outlines a road map you can follow, you can't ignore the message. He has thousands and thousands of testimonials to back up his work, which is being played out worldwide.

When we grow life, our health has got to be at the forefront of any life which has committed to growth. Without health, you become a prisoner inside your body, trapped until it can heal itself. Most people don't think of health as something you grow, yet as you change, so must grow your health. Nothing in this world stays the same it is continually changing.

When we can align our health and our life's growth, we will never become a victim inside our lives.

When we apply **The Habit of Health**, it comes down to one word: responsibility. The growth of your life and your health is in your hands. We become fully engaged inside our lives and are always monitoring how we feel. This is critical as we grow life.

I have a choice I can live in health care or sick care!

Afterword

The great thing about life is we get to choose the type of life we live and grow through our actions. Each experience and path are different as each snowflake. We all live; we all grow; we all die. The growing is where the opportunity lies to become anything to go anywhere to love everything.

If we watch everything, then we become a bystander at the side of life. We can watch the snowfall from the window or go outside and grow a snowman. It is a simple choice!

Growing anything in life takes time, it takes effort, and you might have to roll up your sleeves and get a little messy along the way. Maybe your circumstances at the beginning of life weren't the best, but that should never dictate the kind of life you live. Look at Oprah Winfrey and Nelson Mandela as examples of mastery of growth of life.

We have never lived in a better time to be alive than right now. Compared to one hundred two hundred or one thousand years ago, we are living in Disneyland. We are free to grow. We are free to use the technology we have at our fingertips. We are free to discover the world.

These are the privileges of the twenty-first century.

Stop Growing Old in Life becomes your strating point.

The 8 Habits to Grow Life are the foundation for a more profound realization that all aspects of life can be growing. It is easy to grow when you are young, yet for some reason, that strategy changes as we get older. We go from growing to aging, and when that happens, it is hard to see another side of life.

Growing life is our birthright. It can only stop when you decide for it to stop. If you are doing what you were meant to do in life, why would you ever stop growing your life?

Cheers Brian Jones

Brian Jones Books

Longevity Starts Now!
Life Happens now what the FXCK
Homo Sapien Bob
(Episode 1)
Thailand The First Ten Years

All books can be found on Amazon or where you buy books in **eBook soft cover** and **audible Pick up a copy today!**

www.ingramcontent.com/pod-product-compliance
Lightning Source LLC
Chambersburg PA
CBHW071503070426
42452CB00041B/2278